Lois—
With my
loving thanks for
your loving.
leadership.
God bless you.
Sara

The Smart Gal's Guide *thru* Divorce

"What Lawyers don't tell you."

Sara A.

Co-contributor Sandra D.

WESTBOW
PRESS®
A DIVISION OF THOMAS NELSON
& ZONDERVAN

Scripture taken from the Holy Bible, NEW INTERNATIONAL VERSION®. Copyright © 1973, 1978, 1984 by Biblica, Inc. All rights reserved worldwide. Used by permission. NEW INTERNATIONAL VERSION® and NIV® are registered trademarks of Biblica, Inc. Use of either trademark for the offering of goods or services requires the prior written consent of Biblica US, Inc

WestBow Press books may be ordered through booksellers or by contacting:

WestBow Press
A Division of Thomas Nelson & Zondervan
1663 Liberty Drive
Bloomington, IN 47403
www.westbowpress.com
1 (866) 928-1240

Front Cover Image Copyright: Songchai W/Shutterstock.com

ISBN: 978-1-5127-3362-4 (sc)
ISBN: 978-1-5127-3363-1 (hc)
ISBN: 978-1-5127-3361-7 (e)

Library of Congress Control Number: 2016903816

Print information available on the last page.

WestBow Press rev. date: 11/14/2016

To my Dad and my Mom.
They married once and forever.
And now they are together in Heaven.
Unforgettable.
They believed in Marriage.
And so do I.

SM

*"Now to God who is able
to do immeasurably more
than all we ask or imagine,
according to
His power
that is at work within us."*

The Bible
Ephesians
Chapter 3
Verse 20
NIV

My Acknowledgements

Along the journey. We influence each other.
One to another.

In the journey of this book, I am thankful for those who have encouraged me. Many have agreed with my vision, that this book is needed. In order to meet the need.

I have been inspired to write this book on purpose,
for the greater good.

My deepest thanks to my daughter. You are now an adult and a lovely lady. Thank you, sweet daughter, for your love and encouraging words, always speaking confidence into me. You are amazing. Most especially, thank you for your prayers. I love you. Always.

Also my warmest appreciation to my son-in-law, married to my daughter. You are highly intelligent, steady and faithful. You make my daughter smile. Thank you for your caring words throughout my book writing process. You are very important to me.

Thank you to my mentor, Lois. You are faithful, prayerful and wise.

Thank you to my editor, Sharon Roe. You've got talent.
You were the right one for this editing assignment.

With my thanks to my co-contributor, Sandra. We've been friends since 7th grade, and you are a faithful friend. Plus, you are a smart lady. Friends forever.

My thanks to God, who is over-all. Praying on purpose. I seek to follow God as my guide. Guiding me through, step by step. Moving forward on purpose.

The Smart Gal's Guide *thru* Divorce
"What Lawyers don't tell you."

- Contents -

"Over 25 Key-Areas of Concern"
"The 30 Most-Costly Mistakes"
Contact Information for
Divorce Buddys
Contact Information for
Sara A., Keynote Speaker

The Smart Gal's

Guiding

- Chapter 1 -

Life brings change, and we all live and learn.

For most of us, of course, we never expected that life would bring us into the journey of divorce. We all believed that our dreams would come true.

But instead, sometimes, we find that divorce may come into our lives.

I still believe in marriage.
And I believe that marriage is God's best plan.

But if you're reading this book, and if you're considering a divorce, be thoughtful to consider and reconsider if a divorce is necessary for you and your husband. Reconciliation is always best whenever reconciliation is possible. Seek wise counsel and pray for your best direction.

This book provides a look ahead at the complexities of divorce.

To explain the divorce process and point to important key areas to be sure you consider. This book is written to help you become well-informed and suggest ways to limit the financial losses.

This book is not about me. This book is to guide you.

A guide-book to show you how to get through a tough time. The ones who are equipped to help others are the ones who have lived it and learned it.

I know divorce.
You may wonder, "But how?"

Here's how.
I have become well-informed through the depth of experience that I have gained through my journey of divorce.
I have lived it and learned it.

I have been divorced two times.
Ouch. That hurts.

- Two times. I have hired a Family Law Attorney.
- Two times. I have thought through the many complexities of divorce.
- Two times. I have gathered documents and prayed and looked for my best solutions.
- Two times. I have signed the final Divorce Decree.

This has been my school of divorce. Many lessons learned.

Who could guide you?
Who could inform you?

The one who has lived it and learned it.
This is a guide-book to give you the benefits of my
insider-thinking.

As I am your guide, Sara, along with my co-contributor,
Sandra, we understand what you're going through and what's
up ahead. The many complexities.

We call it "Divorce Dizziness."

Divorce Dizziness is our unique way to put into words the
complexities of the journey of divorce.

The discovery, the documents, the details and the delays.

We are not professional Lawyers.
We are not professional Counselors.
We are not CPAs or CFOs or financial advisors.
But, we are very smart regarding the journey of divorce.
With this guide-book, you will gain over sixteen chapters of
smarts.

Smart thinking, with the potential to save you thousands as
you move forward through the journey.

We provide insider-thinking.
We know what most lawyers don't tell you.
We know "Over 25 Key-Areas of Concern" to make sure you
consider. We know "The 30 Most-Costly Mistakes" to avoid.

With time, step by step, you will get through this journey.
You will find that the divorce dizziness will pass.
There are new days ahead.

We know what you're going through and what's up ahead.
This is the smart gal's guide.

We think it thru with you.
Smart thinking. Smart you.

SM

The Smart Gal's

Calendaring

- Chapter 2 -

- Are you considering a Divorce?
- Or are you in the beginning stages of a Divorce?
- Are you in a time of Separation?
- Or have you already filed for a Divorce?
- Have you been served with a Petition for Divorce?
- Or are you under Temporary Orders for a Divorce?

Wherever you are in the process, we are here to help.

When the impact of divorce comes into life,
we understand that it may feel overwhelming at times.
The questions and concerns may cause us to feel a bit dizzy.
The discovery, the documents, the details and the delays.
Yes, we call it "Divorce Dizziness."
Be assured that you will get through this.
One day at a time.

This kind of "Dizziness" will last only for a season.
You've been thinking about what to do next.
Considering your options.

And seeking your best answers.
Feeling a bit puzzled on how to move forward.
This is a good time to begin to take note.
This chapter will introduce you to what we refer to as
"Calendaring."
Let us explain.

During this time, your thoughts are full with the rush of daily
tasks, endless details and a to-do list of specifics.
You will find days will fly by. And your days may become
more like a "blurrrr."
Step by step, you will get through this.
And calendaring will help you get there.

Here's a tool to keep it all together.

Calendaring

Be equipped with a calendar dedicated to this ONE specific
function.

"Calendaring" will be your dedicated tool to help you keep
track of the divorce process. Your calendar will keep the
details of the divorce organized for your reference.

Here's Why

For most of us, when in a time of change or during a time
of concern, we'll call our mother, or sister or brother or best
friend. Good idea.
Those close to you care about you and can be a very important
shoulder to lean on. We all need to call on someone that we
can depend on to help us through life's challenges. Family is a
great place to get some help!

This reminds me of one of our Divorce Buddys.
We'll call her Hope. (Hope is a fictitious name.)

At Divorce Buddys, we guide women through the complexities of divorce.

Hope had been trying to hold her marriage together for a long time. After years of a troubled marriage, one day, Hope came to her conclusion. Her marriage was broken beyond repair. Hope decided that the condition of her marriage had reached a point that was too hurtful and too unhealthy for her to continue. But Hope did not know where to go from there.
She did not know where to begin.

Hope turned to her sister.
Whenever Hope called on her sister for help,
it was a good call.
Her sister listened to the variety of concerns and Hope's sister always cares.
We all need that kind of help from a sister or a friend.

It's a natural benefit that Hope would feel better after her long talk, because she shared her tears, her fears and various comments of concern.
Hope expressed her thoughts and received some comfort.

But Hope needs more than that.
After her phone call is over, how should Hope continue from that point?

Hope is best equipped to "Calendar" her concerns.
We call it "Calendaring".

We recommend Hope list her concerns during her discussions
in order to keep a more accurate recall list.
On her calendar, Hope should take notes and reflect on the
suggestions she gains from her sister. Hope can later revisit
her list of questions and consult with the right professionals in
order to discover her best answers.

This new dedicated calendar is a smart tool.
Any full-sized calendar will work that is scheduled for
the current year, but we recommend you purchase a new
calendar with a full-sized display page. Even if this new
calendar started a few months past, don't be bothered
about the calendar start date. Just begin to calendar
beginning now.

This Calendaring will provide a reference tool to walk with
you through the process. You will take notes to plan ahead,
put thoughts into action and keep track of your appointments
and deadlines.

Take Note

Calendar the Dates of the Legal Progress

Calendar your critical information by using your calendar to
journal the key dates in your divorce process.
We recommend that you calendar all events that relate to
the progress of your divorce for your future reference and
recall.

Calendar the Legal Process

1. Calendar your appointments with your Lawyer. Note the length of the appointment time to compare to the billing statement.

2. Calendar all Paralegal phone discussions. Note the length of time for each call with the paralegal to compare to the billing statement.

3. Calendar the dates for your Court Filings.

4. Calendar the dates for your Court Motions.

5. Calendar your deadlines set by the Court.

Calendar to Keep Note of your Legal Costs

6. Calendar your attorney's Retainer Fees paid. Note the amount, payment type and date paid.

7. Calendar the additional Legal Fees paid. Note the amount, payment type and date paid.

Calendar to Keep a Note of any Conflicts

8. Calendar any Phone Conversations of Conflict.

9. Calendar any Verbal In-person Conflicts.

10. Calendar any Verbal Threats.

11. Calendar Child Visitation notes: Parenting Conflicts, Scheduling Conflicts.

Calendar your Child's Events

12. Calendar Child's Visitation schedule.

13. Calendar Child's Counseling appointments.

14. Calendar Child's Events, school, sports or practices.

15. Calendar Child's Costs, school, extra-curricular, or medical expenses.

This private calendar should be at your access for notes at all times.

Our Suggestion for Storing

Keep your calendar private and concealed.
Store in an easy to find zippered business tote. Your calendar should travel with you everywhere you go, to allow you to be calendar-ready at all times for adding notes and for your reference.

If you prefer to use an electronic calendar, (via phone, iPad etc.) just be sure your calendar remains private and you still have the easy access of adding notes to the dates.
However, we recommend the traditional paper calendar is best for reference.

With this smart "Calendaring" system, you will have a valuable tool:

- To help remain on schedule with Court Deadlines.
- To help track your Legal Fees spent.
- To help journal times of Conflict.
- To help as a timeline of Parenting Schedule.
- To help track Child's Expenses.

With our plan, we recommend that you use
THIS calendar ONLY for your divorce journey.
This will help you stay on track.

At your fingertips, Calendaring will be a smart reference.
To help you move forward.
Step by step.

Disclaimer: Although this book may provide information and opinions regarding the divorce process, this author and it's contributors and Divorce Buddys do not provide professional legal, financial or mental health counseling. Please consult a trained professional for these matters.

Notes To Remember

_____

_____

_____

_____

_____

_____

_____

_____

_____

_____

_____

_____

_____

The Smart Gal's

Lawyering

- Chapter 3 -

Now that you have a good start with Calendaring, let's talk Lawyers.

In life, step by step, we move forward every day into new life experiences. We are always looking at our options and shopping to find the best choices. Looking for the very best choice at every turn.

Consider the many ways we shop and consider when we are hunting to find our best buy.

Consider these:

- When you are shopping for the best car.
- Or when you are researching to buy the best home.

We take the time to compare prices, ask for opinions, and look to read the reviews. We think it through, and look at all of the choices.

We all want to consider our options.
Am I right?

In America, our legal system is our man-made civilized
process for settling disputes. We need our lawyers to process
our disputes in a civilized fashion.
In the case of a divorce, we agree that the lawyer leads the
legal process.

Here again, we need to go shopping and consider our options.

Be aware that lawyers practice in a wide range of legal
specialties. We need to seek out the best attorney to handle
these legal matters of divorce.

The Lawyer's Area of Practice

Lawyers may specialize in:

- Estate Planning
- Patents and Trademarks
- Business Law
- Personal Injury
- Bankruptcy Law
- Tax Law
- Criminal Law
- Family Law
  ... To name a few.

We recommend your lawyer's primary focus and expertise
should be with Family Law. With experience in the family
court. The family law attorney knows the details about divorce
and he/she knows the court system including the options, the
detours and the potential for delays.

Seek to hire your very best Family Law Attorney.

Smart Lawyering

We will continue here to refer to our client, Hope, our divorce buddy.

Let's learn from Hope.

Now in regards to Lawyering ...

When Hope realized that a divorce was necessary, she called her brother for advice, and he offered his help. But even with her brother's good intentions, he did not know very much about divorce. He didn't have any first-hand experience with it.

Hope's brother wanted to help, so he turned to the web to search for an attorney to help his sister. He searched to find an attorney with a good reputation.
Thinking about his options and thinking about possible resources for reference, he also asked his co-workers, his neighbors, and his trusted friends to see if they could recommend a divorce attorney. He did his best.

Your family members will have the best intentions to help, and they may be able to help you find a good lawyer. But you need to make sure your attorney is your best choice, your smart choice.

Here are some other elements to consider when selecting your legal counsel.

A Smart Plan to Seek Legal Representation

Consider the following elements in making the selection for your legal representation.

Select Lawyers to Interview

Here is the place to begin your next step forward.

Interview a minimum of three family law attorneys.
You may consider interviewing as many as five family law attorneys. The more lawyers to interview, the more you will learn and gain a sense of what feels right to you.

Consider the following when selecting Lawyers to interview:

1. The lawyer's area of legal specialty –
   To be a Family Law Attorney.

2. A board certified lawyer.

3. A member of the Bar Association.

4. The number of years practicing law.

5. Check to review if there are any penalties on his/her professional record.

6. Consider the convenience of the office location and the business image of the lawyer's practice.

7. How do you react to the size of the law firm?
   A single attorney?
   A team of attorneys?
   With support staff?
   One paralegal or more?

It's always smart to choose a Board Certified Family Law Attorney. Your lawyer needs to have acquired experience, should be well-known and recognized in the court of law in your district court. A lawyer with a good reputation will be held in high regard with the locally elected judges.
With an experienced family law attorney, he/she will know the judges on the bench in your district court. And he/she will have experience with the judge's track record, judicial posturing and how the judge may lean on your divorce issues.

Begin by contacting well-established family law attorneys. Call their office to request a divorce consultation.
Ask the office receptionist if there will be consultation fee and ask for the cost.

Some family law attorneys will charge for the initial consultation and many will not. Consider this initial cost when setting up your interview process.
If there is an interview cost, we recommend that you accept their fee as a worthwhile small start-up expense. It is important to know that you have considered all of your best possible candidates.

Begin interviewing various divorce attorneys right away.
It will take time to select your legal counsel.
We find it is best to schedule two interviews in the same day, back to back.
This creates a benefit to compare one to the other plus the time-saving organization of two interviews in the same day. Double book the day. Smart.

Soon you will find the best legal counsel to fit your style for the direction of your divorce.

Interview Questions

At each interview, you will want to ask the lawyer
the following:

1. Number of years practicing Family Law in the current
   court jurisdiction.

2. Hourly rate for the Attorney.

3. Hourly rate for their Paralegal.

4. Ask for the lawyer's recommendation for your next step
   of action, and the overall direction he/she recommends
   to follow in the divorce process. Ask for their opinion
   regarding the mediation process.

5. As their client, how often can you expect to meet with
   the lawyer for an update?

6. As their client, how will you communicate, through
   phone appointments or email?

7. Ask for the amount of the initial Retainer fee
   (initial dollars) required to begin.

8. Billing Statements:
   Will you receive monthly billing statements?
   Will the statement reference the tasks performed as
   related to the hours billed?
   Will the statements be sent by mail or by email?

9. If all retainer fees are not entirely spent, will the
   retainer dollars remaining in your account be returned
   to you?

Idea:
When you have decided to move forward to sign
their agreement for legal representation, you may
consider asking for the courtesy to wave their initial
consultation fee.

Your Family Law Attorney

By now you are making progress.

After you select your family law attorney, there will be a legal
contract to sign for legal representation and a legal retainer
fee will be required.
Typical retainer fees range from $1,000 to $10,000.
We suggest that you consider paying your retainer fees by
using your joint married credit card. Your legal expenses
from your divorce are a marital expense, and the divorce
cost should be considered a marital debt in your divorce
negotiations.

You are ready to move forward.

The next step begins with filing for divorce.
Who files first? He or She?
Filed in what county?
The divorce will be filed in your local county jurisdiction, and
a local judge will be assigned to your case through the court
system.

What is the Reason or the Grounds for the Divorce Petition?

In Texas, Grounds for Divorce may include:

- **Insupportability** - The court may grant a divorce without regard to fault if the marriage has become insupportable because of discord or conflict of personalities that destroys the legitimate ends of the marital relationship and prevents any reasonable expectation of reconciliation.

- **Cruelty** - The court may grant a divorce in favor of one spouse if the other spouse is guilty of cruel treatment toward the complaining spouse of a nature that renders further living together insupportable.

- **Adultery** - The court may grant a divorce in favor of one spouse if the other spouse has committed adultery.

- **Conviction of Felony** - The court may grant a divorce in favor of one spouse if during the marriage the other spouse has been convicted of a felony.

- **Abandonment** - The court may grant a divorce in favor of one spouse if the other spouse left the complaining spouse and remained away for at least one year with the intention of abandonment.

- **Living Apart** - The court may grant a divorce in favor of either spouse if the spouses have lived apart without cohabitation for at least three years.

- **Confinement** – The court may grant a divorce when a spouse is held in confinement in a mental hospital.

These are listed as grounds for divorce in Texas, and may not be listed in entirety.

Delivery of the Divorce Petition

If you have filed for divorce, your spouse will be served divorce papers, the Petition for divorce.

Here is a question to consider.

If You are the One Filing for the Divorce -

If you are the one filing for the Divorce, you are referred to as the "Petitioner."
Consider where it is best for your spouse to be served the divorce petition papers.
To be served while at work, at their business office?
This may create an uncomfortable scene.
Consider their reaction and response when served with the divorce petition paperwork at their office.
Or
If you are living apart and currently separated, you may prefer to have your spouse served with the divorce papers at their separate residence.

Your goal is to fulfill the necessary legal process and protocol. No need to stir up trouble or cause public embarrassment.

Or If You are the One on the Other Side –

It is possible that you may be the one who has been served with the divorce petition. In this case, you are receiving this paperwork and you will be referred to as the "respondent" in the divorce case.

As the respondent, you will need to respond in writing to the divorce petition within a set time period. We recommend that you seek to hire a Family Law Attorney for legal counsel.

If you fail to respond to the divorce petition, within the allotted time, there may be a default filed against you. The default could later be presented to the judge at a default hearing. If you have not responded to the court within the time deadline, your spouse may possibly be granted an advantage for requests in court, due to your lack of response within protocol.

After the divorce petition is filed, there is most often a court ordered waiting period that must be satisfied. Your divorce may not be granted until complying with the laws in your state.

From state to state across the United States, there is a wide variation of time restraints.

Here are some examples to highlight this variance.
For your reference, at the time of this published writing:

- In Texas, there is a sixty day waiting period.
- In Colorado, there is a ninety day waiting period before the divorce may be granted.
- In the state of New Hampshire, there is no waiting period for the court to grant the divorce.

Every state has their state-defined specific laws for the divorce timeline and procedure.

After your divorce has been filed in court, we believe it is to your benefit to file for Temporary Orders.

Temporary Orders is a legal term.

Temporary Orders are created to make an interim agreement while the divorce case is pending.

Temporary Orders may include but are not limited to agreement for payments of spousal support, child support, child visitation, debts, attorney's fees, child custody or conservatorship to name a few.

Moving Forward

Throughout the sequence of events in the divorce process, we recommend the benefits of a divorce coach. A divorce coach is informed to guide you through the wide range of considerations in the journey of divorce.

Read on to our next chapter to learn more about a divorce coach. So that you will consider how to become better informed.

Smart thinking. Smart you.

Disclaimer: Although this book may provide information and opinions regarding the divorce process, this author and it's contributors and Divorce Buddys do not provide professional legal, financial or mental health counseling. Please consult a trained professional for these matters.

Notes To Remember

The Smart Gal's

Divorce Coaching

- Chapter 4 -

The Divorce Coach is an emerging concept that has been created to meet the need.

Across America, the divorce coach is quickly becoming a new smart tool for those who find themselves in the journey of divorce.

At Divorce Buddys, we are recognized as Certified Divorce Coaches. We are inspired to guide women through the journey of divorce. We think it through with you.
We explain the divorce process and discuss a variety of options.

We know the business-side of divorce.
We empower women to become well-informed regarding the complexities of divorce. The considerations, the options and how to avoid potential costly detours. We prepare you with key information ahead of time at a fraction of the cost.

We Agree

The Lawyer leads the Legal Process

We recognize that the lawyer is specially trained and educated to perform the legal protocol as well as being especially skilled to handle the court filings and the document creation. The lawyer is knowledgeable to document complex issues including child custody concerns, division of assets and division of debts. The lawyer is known to conduct his/her business with a professional business-like manner while processing the legal matters with the court on behalf of his/her client.

The attorney, along with his paralegal and/or legal assistant will direct the legal matters that encompass key elements involved however may not address many of the remaining life complexities of a divorce. With a divorce coach, clients will become better informed regarding a broad range of concerns and unknown complex considerations.

Wherever you may be in the process, a divorce coach will prepare you with key information ahead of time in order for you to make your very best decisions.

Remember Hope? We call her Hope.
She is looking ahead at her rocky road of questions and concerns. Her emotions are spinning. We are here to be her divorce coach, her divorce buddy. Do you know someone like Hope?

Again, we call her Hope, using this fictitious persona, because our clients' names and information remain confidential.

Hope turned to Divorce Buddys for information at a fraction of the cost. Hope trusts Divorce Buddys because she has seen our commitment to our "Golden Seal of Trust". Hope is seeking to make sure she makes her best decisions with her family law attorney. Step by step, Hope calls on Divorce Buddys, when she realizes that she needs to learn more about her next step forward.

Divorce involves a wide range of considerations while in the legal process. With Divorce Buddys, Hope is offered a wealth of information.

Together We Review

"Over 25 Key-Areas of Concern" to be sure to consider. (See Reference Tools provided in this book.)

"The 30 Most-Costly Mistakes" to avoid. (See Reference Tools provided in this book.)

With Divorce Buddys, we suggest wise divorce strategies with the potential to save our clients thousands. We provide valuable wisdom to help control the legal losses through the divorce process. To help meet a wide range of needs, we are able to suggest from our list of approved vendors, Selective Referrals.

A Wide Range of Selective Referrals

Including:

- Family Law Attorneys
- Financial Advisors
- Income Tax Advisors
- Mediators
- Estate Planning Attorneys
- Qualified Retirement Analysts, Retirement Plan, QDRO
- Realtors to Re-Locate, Buy, Sell or Rent
- Packing & Moving Companies, Storage, Locksmiths

- Private Security Guard Companies
- Insurance Providers
- Resume and LinkedIn Career Services
- Career Coaches
- Professional Counselors for Adults and for Children

We have written this guide-book to put our smarts into writing. We call it insider-thinking.
There is much we have learned about the divorce process. We have the potential to save our clients thousands.

We are inspired to guide women through the journey.
We help you through what we call "Divorce Dizziness."
We discuss the many considerations and complexities involved.
The discovery, the documents, the details and the delays.

We know what you're going through and what's up ahead.
We guide our clients through to divorce recovery.
"We think it thru with you."

Notes To Remember

Notes To Remember

The Smart Gal's

Learning the Divorce Process

- Chapter 5 -

By choosing to read this book and opening these pages, you are seeking information that will help you make your best decisions.

In order to make your best decisions, it's best to gain information from someone who has been there.
Someone experienced.

And here is a necessary truth for you.
Are you ready?

A Truth: A Divorce is a Lawsuit

Take time to sit back and take this in.

Divorce is a legal matter, recognized by the state operating within the United States of America.
A divorce is the dissolution of the marriage certificate.

A divorce is cancelling the legal duties and responsibilities within a marriage and dissolving the bonds of matrimony between a married couple.

Divorce is a lawsuit. A necessary truth.
Ouch. We know. This can hurt.

By reading this book, you are getting better informed to guide you through.

After you complete this chapter on
"Learning the Divorce Process," you will have a better overview of where you are now and what's up ahead.

In the journey of divorce, in order to seek the best possible outcome, we agree that the lawyer leads the legal process. We recommend selecting a family law attorney. (Refer to Chapter 3, Lawyering.)

Divorce proceedings generally include the following.
Here is a general overview of the process.
(This is not to be considered a complete listing of variations or a complete listing of court ordered procedures.)

Filing the Petition

A divorce begins with the petition.
This may be referred to as a "complaint" in some states.
This petition informs the court and serves your spouse with the legal filing to end your marriage.

Response to Petition

After the other has been served papers, he/she is entitled to file opposing papers.

Temporary Orders

Temporary Orders is the legal document created to set into place the rules to follow while the divorce case is in process and is currently pending.

Either spouse can request Temporary Orders and these orders may designate and/or define a range of issues including who will stay in the residence, spousal support, financial responsibilities and who is responsible for the children during this interim time, to name a few.

Discovery Process

Discovery is a legal term for the legal process of obtaining information about the other spouse.

This legal term is called the discovery process.

The discovery process may become lengthy and complex when emotions are allowed to continue to extend the process.

Here are examples of Discovery tools:

    a. Documents – Request for production of documents.

    b. Interrogatories – Written questions requiring a written answer.

    c. Depositions – Spouse, others and/or experts are required to answer questions under oath.

    d. Subpoena – To seek information, evidence from a named deponent to give a testimony or to gain production of documents or both. A deponent is someone making a deposition under oath.

Mediation Process

The mediation process is for the opposing spouses to negotiate and seek to reach an agreement for the wide range of divorce issues. Mediation is a legal process and a legal expense. Mediation is often found to be a less expensive approach than to proceed with the back and forth process between the lawyers written motions, requests and communications. This back and forth may be referred to as "papering." Papering is the revolving requests for documentation used for posturing their client's best interest.

In contrast, mediation is designed to discontinue and shorten the discovery process and to move to negotiate in order to arrive at a compromise and an agreement. At the mediation table, there may be a power-play by one or by the other spouse, claiming to refuse to compromise on various issues.

Generally, the mediation costs include the hourly fees for each of the family law attorneys providing legal counsel for each side while on location. There are additional fees for the Mediator, who is contracted for a half-day or a full-day in order to lead the mediation effort. Even though this day will be costly, while gathered at a meeting on-site and working in close proximity, there is pressure to negotiate and great potential and expectation to make progress. To work to create a negotiated mediated agreement.

The Mediation Process Includes:

- Your Family Law Attorney, On-site. Hourly fees.
- His Family Law Attorney, On-site. Hourly fees.
- Mediator, On-site. Additional Half-day / Full-day fees to be divided.

Often the total cost for the mediation process can be a significant savings by way of preventing a prolonged escalation of legal documents, interjected delays and additional fees. Mediation has the potential goal to bring compromise in order to arrive at an agreement necessary to produce the final divorce decree.

Negotiated Settlement

A divorce settlement is a negotiated agreement of division for the final divorce decree. An agreeable settlement provides the benefit of privacy, preventing marital issues from being debated openly in the courtroom. It is most beneficial for both parties to come to a mutual agreement rather than imposing a judgment to be dictated by a judge while in court and being subject to the judge's ruling.

Most family law attorneys make recommendations to avoid trial by a judge and work to help their clients arrive at a divorce agreement and arrive at a settlement.

With every legal case, the courtroom requires certain legal procedures that must be strictly followed to meet proper procedures for the final judgment to be granted. Your lawyer will be performing the legal process with documentation to satisfy the legal protocol, guidelines and court ordered requirements.

The lawyer cannot and is not in control of making your decisions.

Once the divorce agreement has been settled, it is documented, created and filed with the court. Then, it is up to both parties involved to follow the divorce decree with a willing compliance. It is far too expensive to return to the legal process to legally enforce the various details of the agreed upon divorce decree.

Following the divorce granted, follow the divorce agreement in order to avoid future legal battles and avoid additional financial losses returning to court.

Going to Trial

Every trial is expensive.
We do not recommend taking your divorce petition to trial.
If a negotiated divorce agreement is not produced, a petition for divorce will be forced to go to trial. When in trial, under oath, you and your spouse would be asked for your testimony along with other selected witnesses, supported by numerous documents referred to as "exhibits."

Any case going to trial is an expensive legal process.

Following the presentation of information in trial, through documentation, testimony and cross examination, the judge would then be the one to decide upon the division that will dictate your divorce. We have found in divorce proceedings, when forced to go to trial, most decisions are declared by the judge, rather than by a jury.

Following trial, each party may appeal the judge's ruling and appeal to a higher court. An appeal will bring additional legal expense to the divorce process.

Smart Pointers

Here is valuable information that comes to you through our miles of experience.

Every Divorce Decree requires Compromise

Without compromise, your case will be forced to be taken to trial and the judge will be placed in the position to decide and to divide. And in a trial, your divisions will be dictated by the judge.

Why not compromise? We recommend that the opposing parties compromise to find agreement in order to avoid the huge losses of taking a divorce petition to the judge and multiplying additional court costs. It is always uncertain how the judge will rule in each case.

Best to find compromise and seek to prevent your case from going to trial.

The journey of divorce is a long process. We recommend that you give much thought to your list of priorities and find places where you can offer compromise.

List Your Priorities

In Order of Your Priority

You decide your priorities. This is simply a list of categories for you to begin your thinking process about your ranking of your priorities.

1. Your Financial Needs.

2. Your Material Possessions Needed and Necessary.

3. Your Material Possessions desired that hold Sentimental Value.

4. Your Child's Needs / Children's Needs.

5. Your Debts.

6. Your Career Needs.

7. Your Relocation Issues. Current residence. Stay, Sell, Buy, Rent, Relocate.

8. Your Legal Fees. Total Dollars willing to spend on this legal process in order to achieve your list of Priorities. ... To name a few.

Set Smart Priorities

With a long list of needs, hopes and wishes, your lawyer's billable hours will be adding up to negotiate each issue on your behalf.

With the tensions continuing throughout the negotiations, you will accumulate higher legal fees. Hour by hour.
It is best to write out your long list of wishes. And put them into a sequence of your priority.
Ask for all of your wishes in the divorce division, including all of your hopes and begin to negotiate and compromise from there. Be ready to give and concede some of your wishes but negotiate to hold to your priorities.

With your complete list of initial requests for financial assets, possessions, and child support issues, you will have a better outcome by preparing to relinquish some of your optional priorities while you are in the negotiation process.

Here is our Smart Strategy to consider:

Ask for it all.
And then begin to compromise.
Prepare to release your optional points. Gradually.
And you win.

But, how do I win?

Why does this plan of giving-in with compromising work for me?

Here's How YOU Often Benefit

Gradually, as you release your optional points, your
"Soon-to-be-Ex" will be pleased, winning each optional point
over to his side.
But you, hold tight to your Priorities.
Set your focus on your most highly-held priority issues.
Ask for it all.
And be ready to release and relinquish each item you can yield
in compromise. One at a time.
As you calculate a response to His negotiations,
hold on to Your Priorities.
To compromise and to find agreement will help control the
legal fees from escalating.

Here are two fictitious examples:

- It may be wise for Hope to ask for an increased
  monthly child support income as her priority and as
  a compromise, perhaps she may be willing to yield on
  accepting a portion of the joint marital financial debt.

- It may be Hope's choice to negotiate strongly for her
  release from a sizeable financial debt, and as her
  compromise, be willing to comply and agree to His
  request for His plan for joint custody regarding his
  child visitation scheduling wishes.

We are informing you that it is in this compromising that you
will win. Because you will limit your billable hours and control
your legal fees and expenses. Yes, you will be relinquishing
some points, but stand firm to accomplish your priority needs.

Try to be sure your priorities are not set on a revengeful basis but
your choices rest on your priority ranking. It does not work well

to battle over one point merely out of anger or in resentment. In order to limit your legal fees, it requires compromise. Focus on your priority list and negotiate on the rest.

A lengthy standoff of opposition is far too costly!

With conflict in divorce, the lawyers are the ones who will win your money with their legal representation, their mounting billable hours for negotiation and settlement. With a lengthy battle, the lawyers win more of your family nest egg.

In summary, we recommend that you create your complete list of hopes, needs, wishes and priorities and negotiate from there.

Stand strong for your top priorities.
Compromise and let go of some hopes and wishes.
You will always know that you did your best.

You are smarter today than you were yesterday.
Better informed.
Smart you. Smart move.
Moving forward.

Notes To Remember

Notes To Remember

The Smart Gal's

Documenting

- Chapter 6 -

You have heard the phrase,
Now that is "worth its weight in gold."

This phrase describes the great value of gold.
We can agree that gold is a precious metal and a treasure.
Gold often holds our rubies, our emeralds and our diamonds.
Our precious gems.
Ahhh, yes, the beauty of solid gold.

Valuable. Gold. To have and to hold.

Here is our way of explaining a valuable truth.

It is important to recognize all of your valuables.
To recognize the value of your credit history.
Your credit history needs to be documented and kept in a safe place. Your financial documentation is a treasure.

(Our most precious treasures are our children. Of course.
Our children are the most valuable and priceless.)

Now, back to my point:
Here is our explanation of this application.
It is very important to document all of your valuables.

Your financial documents are worth more than their
weight in gold.

Your credit history is your paper trail of credit worthiness.
Your documents carry a strong influence on your divorce
process and in the division of your assets and debts.

You need to document your finances in order to discover and
define your current financial position.

If you are currently married, these documents are a part
of your marital union. We recommend that you make a
copy of all the financial documents to create an accurate
representation of your financial "state of the union."

Compile all the financial documents in order to piece together
your financial history and create a financial track record. By
clarifying your credit history, you will become well informed
on how to move forward.

Your documents will define your credit history and may be
considered more precious than gold.

Your Credit History

A Compilation of the following:

- Your Income
- Your Income Tax Statements
- Your Mortgage
- Your Property Taxes
- Your Bank Loans
- Your Credit Cards
- Your Retirement Funds, IRA
- Your Investments

- How about His Credit?
- His Income
- His Income Tax Statements
- His Retirement Funds, IRA
- His Investments

Your future depends on getting this right.
Solid documentation.
Your documents influence your financial future.
Your documents may be worth more than their weight in gold.

Your Documents

Financial and Legal Documents may include:

- Bank Statements
- Mortgage Documents
- Home Equity Loans
- Home Appraisal
- Property Taxes/Statements

- IRA Statements
- Car Loans
- Income Tax Returns
- Employment Income / Track-Record
- Official Documents
- Social Security, Both His and Hers
- Last Will & Testament
- Birth Certificates for All
- History Tracking of Finances, Movement, Transfers
- Cell Phone Account Ownership, Billing and Rights
- Credit Card Account Numbers
- Credit Card Financial Limits
- Credit Card Balances and Bills
- Debt Balances
- Loans
- Frequent Flyer Miles
- Legal Documents and Legal Filings
- Papers from your Lawyer

We recommend that you document a history trail, tracking month to month, a financial account of progression as you move forward.

Keep Copies

Copies to Document all Financial Accounts including:

- One year ago, your past records of financial history.
- The previous three months, recent trends.
- Current statements, watching the cash-flow.
- Continue to keep copies to track all financial activity and movement.

We recommend you take good care of these documents. We suggest storing all of these copies in a portable plastic file box.

Your documents will be stored together and easy to find for your reference. Smart thinking.

We know what you're going through and what's up ahead.

Read on to the next chapter to see how "Organizing" your documents can bring valuable benefits.

Moving forward.

Notes To Remember

The Smart Gal's

Organizing

- Chapter 7 -

Life is full of valuable tools made for important tasks.
Tools to get the job done.
Let's talk about tools, and think about the value of
being well-equipped and well-organized.

Think about the tools in your kitchen.
The kitchen is composed of an assortment of essential tools
well-designed to create the meals that we enjoy.
We "go-to" our kitchen tools to make it all happen.

Ladies, we all know about the wide variety of tools that are
stored and ready for our use in the kitchen.

Just think about it. We have tools for measuring, for preparing
and for serving. Every meal is a creation and every meal is
made-to-order using our kitchen tools.

Consider this:

Hope, our divorce buddy, she is an organized lady.

Hope knows her kitchen.

In her kitchen, her dinner plates are stacked and ready in the cabinet. She knows right where they are stored.

She keeps her cooking utensils grouped and easy to find in a utensil drawer. Her tools are organized. And Hope knows where to find them. She can reach for what she needs in a moment's notice.

Just like kitchen tools, Hope has learned to be well-prepared by keeping her documents organized and ready for her to put to good use.

Now, think of the current task that is ahead of you.

The divorce process.

Your divorce process.

You need to be well-equipped.

With the right tools.

- You will need documents to "measure" your financial needs.
- You will need documents to "prepare" the division of your assets.
- You will need to be ready to "serve" files of information to your lawyer.
- Become organized in order to be "well-equipped".

Because we know the journey of divorce, we want you to be aware of the documents you will need to have copied and organized, put into order and placed into files in order to be ready.

Here is how to organize your documents to be well-equipped.

Your File Box

A Plastic Legal File Box

First, we recommend that you buy a plastic file box at a local office supply store.
Plastic construction is much preferred over the crushable cardboard version.

This file box should be large enough to hold the letter-size documents:
8 ½ x 11 paper.
But also a file box size wide enough to hold the larger legal-size documents:
8 ½ x 14 paper.
This plastic file box should have the capability to hang file folders inside the file box in order to keep your document files hanging in place.

Hanging File Folders

As you gather copies of your documents, group those copies by file folders with file names. Your documents will be easy to find, well-organized and stored in your file box.

Document Storage

We recommend that you store your plastic legal file box in the trunk of your car.

Why Store in the Trunk of My Car?

Our suggestion. For your documents to be concealed and out of sight.

Is it possible, your "Soon-to-be-Ex" may come to your home, one day, while you are not there?

Is it possible, your "Soon-to-be-Ex" may see your files of documents and look through your paperwork left in a stack on top of your desk?

Why Conceal these Documents?

Why Out of Sight?

Because you are better prepared when you are well-equipped with your document copies with you, always available and organized for your easy reference and easy access.

This file box holds valuable and confidential financial documents. All to be kept compiled, assembled and in good care, in a safe place and out of sight.

Organizing

Your Documentation

We recommend the following file folders for your organization within your file box:

- Assets File
- Debts File
- Children's Issues File
- Legal Fees Paid File
- Expenses and Receipts File
- Legal Filings and Legal Documents File
- Need-To-Do File
- Reference File
- Misc. File

This will get you started.

With this organization of your documents, stored all in one place and with your compilation of file folders by category, you will be well-equipped with your tools of documentation.

Organized and Ready at your fingertips

- For Your "Go-To" Reference
- For Meetings with Your Lawyer
- For A Resource of Compiled Information
- For Whenever Needed, in a Moment's Notice

Smart you.
Well-equipped.
And moving forward.

Disclaimer: Although this book may provide information and opinions regarding the divorce process, this author and it's contributors and Divorce Buddys do not provide professional legal, financial or mental health counseling. Please consult a trained professional for these matters.

Notes To Remember

_____

_____

_____

_____

_____

_____

_____

_____

_____

_____

_____

_____

_____

_____

_____

_____

The Smart Gal's

Protecting

- Chapter 8 -

We all like to feel well-protected.
It feels good to know that we have planned ahead to do
all that we can.

It's best to protect everything that holds value.
To find ways to prevent potential incidents that may
be avoided.

We think ahead, and we try to plan ahead.

You and Social Media

Interesting ... to consider the phrase, Social Media.
Here is the word, "Social".

When in the journey of the divorce process,
this is NOT the time to be "Social".
Not the time to be "Socializing" over the "Media".

During the journey of your divorce,
We recommend ... No Social Media.

Not Now

No Media, No Posting, No Broadcasting, Not Now

- No Facebook Posts.
- No Facebook Likes/Comments.
- No Birthday Messaging.
- No Blogging.
- No Tweeting.
- No Photos Shared.
- No Instagram.
- No Snapchat.

Let's consider our buddy, Hope.
Should she?
Could she?
Well, she is better off, not. Not now.

- This is not the time to Post a Selfie during a girls-night-out.
- Not a good idea to Post a personal update on Facebook.
- Not the place to Post any anger or sarcasm.
- Not the right time to Post any new love interests.
- Not the time to Post any social parties or plans.

Hope is best protected by keeping a low profile.
By controlling her public view and stopping her social media posts. To maximize her privacy regarding her personal interests.

Texting

Limiting Digital Communications

We have found that texting is a part of our everyday, for all of us. Texting is a helpful communication convenience.
Best to be used for quick thoughts or updates.

It can be tempting to use texting to explain a concern or describe an issue, but best not here. Not now.
Just keep it short. Informational and short.
In this time of juggling divorce issues and concerns via text, it is best to keep texting short and limited.

When in the divorce process, we recommend that texting be used "as needed for information" only.

Brief texts without explanations are best.
Did you know?
All of those texts can be "Discovered" and used as a reference of conduct in a divorce court case.

Stay on the side of innocence so that your texting cannot come back to bite. And by the way, no profanity in texts. This is the time to be at your all-time best behavior. You will be glad every time you think ahead and choose to use self-control.

Keep your Texts G-Rated

- Don't say it (even though He makes you mad).
- Don't reply (even though you know He just lied).
- Don't fight back (even though He is being rude).
- Don't use profanity (even though you are pushed to the limit).

- Don't taunt him (even though He may have some bad news coming soon).

New Account Passwords - Now

Update and change your login codes and your passwords now.

You are better protected by creating new account passwords:

- For Your Credit Card Account On-Line.
- For Your Cell Phone Account.
- For Your Bank Account Login and Password.

Make note of all of these changes for your future reference and your future recall.

Here's An Idea:

Note your new login account information in a dedicated spiral binder of passwords.
Store in your organizing plastic file box.

Or

Note your new login account information along with your Calendaring. To be ready and on-hand in your Calendar for your private reference.

Securing Your Mail - Now

Thinking about Your Mail

1. U.S. Mail
   Rent a New Post Office Box at a local mail center store.

This provides a protected place of Address to receive your Mail:

- New Address to receive your Lawyer's mailed correspondence
- New Address for your personal Credit Card Account and for statements
- New Address for your new Banking / Checking Account

2. Email
   Set up a New Email Address.

   This is a good time for a new email address along with creating a new password. Choose to use your new email address for all of your legal correspondence.

   Do not give this new email address to your "Soon-to-be-Ex".
   Don't give this new email to your old friends.
   Use your old email for your old friends.

   Begin to use a New Email:

   - New Email for your New Interests
   - New Email for your Lawyer's information
   - New Email for your New Banking and Business Accounts

   Step by step. Begin now.

Security-on-Guard

As an Option to Consider

With the gradual division of marital possessions, there may arise a need for your "Soon-to-be-Ex" to pick up some of his additional belongings.

This meeting should be pre-arranged for a pre-set time.

It may be prudent to consider hiring a Security Guard to be on-site for this pick-up meeting. Often, this meeting begins with a calm atmosphere. Both of you may be thinking, "Let's see how this goes". But this is a time when emotions can flare-up. Words can heat-up with emotions on edge.

This is a precaution.
Both of you, the wife and the "Soon-to-be-Ex," are experiencing a time of intense emotion and may sense a challenge for personal gain.

We suggest you consider hiring a professional security guard in uniform, through a certified security company to stand by on-site during a pre-set home-visit.

As women, we often have a gentler, more trusting heart, and a "Soon-to-be-Ex" may wish to control the situation. You will feel strengthened and you will be safer with a security guard, hired, and on-site to observe the interaction and prevent any conflict from developing.

It is best to be protected.

And we want to help you think it through to take protective measures.

To think ahead. To plan ahead.
To move forward.

SM

Notes To Remember

The Smart Gal's

Calculating Finances

- Chapter 9 -

Every dollar counts.
Do you agree?

A banking institution is required to account for every dollar
and reconcile every dollar. In order to balance the accounts.
The banker is responsible for all of the money coming in and
all of the money going out.

I am not a banker. Are you?

But whether or not financial numbers come easily to you, we
all need to pass THIS math test. At home, we have numbers to
crunch. Dollars to tabulate.

We must take the time to know how to calculate our
financial world.

Think It Thru

Financially Speaking

Here is a wealth of information.

By moving forward with Documenting in Chapter 6, followed by Organizing in Chapter 7, you have gathered many important financial documents.

We can help you add it up.

Review our "Charting Finances to Review" that is included at the end of this chapter. Add it up. And make sure everything is considered.

You will want your best answers for these questions. The more accurate your numbers, the more accurate a financial picture you will discover.

By reviewing our outline,
"Charting Finances To Review"
you will see your financial picture more clearly.
This will give you a good gauge.

If for any category, you are not certain about a dollar value, simply enter your best estimate and add a question mark **(?)** following that entry. You will be highlighting that your entered number is only your best estimation for your future reference and consideration.

You are going to discover how much it requires to meet your life's expenses and to keep your home running.

This makes good sense. Dollars and cents.

Okay, we're ready for an overview before we begin.

Overview and Explanation

A Summary of Marital Debts

Money Owed Per Creditor:

Your lawyer will want to know your list of Debts. You need to know:

1. Your Credit Card Debt dollar amount.

   List each Credit Card by each individual Account/Card:
   a. Total Credit Card Balance per Credit Card Account.
   b. Monthly Minimum $$ amount due per Credit Card Account.

   During the divorce process, we do not recommend to pay down your credit card balances. Debts are a shared marital debt.

   We suggest you pay every month the credit card minimum balance and to pay the minimum on-time in order to maintain a clean credit record.

   But we suggest, hold the debt for now, and it will be negotiated and divided in the divorce agreement.

2. Your Residence: Mortgage Loan, Property Rental, Apartment Rental.

   a. Total Loan Value.
   b. Current Loan Balance - Loan responsibility.

3. Your Property Tax Liability, Annual.

4. Additional Loans, Home Equity Loan, Property Loan, Car Loans.

Overview and Explanation

A Summary of Monthly Operating Costs

Home Operating Costs:

- Primary Home Mortgage or Home Rental Cost per Month.
- Property Taxes Cost per Month.
- Home Insurance or Renter's Insurance Cost per Month.
- Home Utilities:
  Electric per Month.
  Gas per Month.
  Water per Month.
  Trash Fee per Month.
  Cell Phone per Month.
  Home Phone per Month.
  Cable TV / Internet Services per Month.
  Security System Monitoring per Month.
  Lawn Care expense per Month.

Transportation Costs:

- Car Payment 1 - per Month (His).
- Car Payment 2 - per Month (Hers).
- Car Payment 3 - per Month (Extra 3rd Car).
- Auto Insurance/per Car/ Monthly.
- Gasoline expense per Month estimate for all Cars.
- Highway Toll Fees.

Personal Care Costs:

- Hair Care per Month.
- Nails/Beauty services per Month estimate.
- Clothing purchases per Month.
- Dry-cleaning cost per Month.

Food Expenses / Costs:

- Groceries per Month.
- Restaurants / Eat-Out / Dine-Out per Month.

Additional Membership Fees / Costs:

- Gym Membership per Month.
- Country Club per Month.

Monthly Child/Children Expenses / Costs:

- School Tuition.
- Sports Fees.
- Lunch School Expense.
- School Uniforms.
- Sports Uniforms.
- Extracurricular Classes.
- Day Care Costs.
- Summer Camp Costs.
- Dental Care.
- Orthodontics Fees.
- Medical Appointments.
- Prescription Costs.
- Clothing Needs.

Overview and Explanation

A Summary of Fluctuating Random Expenses

Medical Expenses:

- Personal Medical Appointments.
- Dental Care.
- Prescription Costs.

Auto Repair Expenses

Home Repair Expenses

Overview and Explanation

A Summary of Marital Assets

Property Equity / Value:

- Primary Home.
- Additional Home.
- Additional Land.

Automobile Equity / Value

Retirement Account QDRO Assets:

- IRA Account / His Total Value.
- IRA Account / Hers Total Value.
- Company Stock Equity, Holdings Total Value.
- Company Annual Bonuses - Per Year, Expectation.
- Life Insurance Policies Value and Expense.
- Social Security Benefits - Year to Begin and Income Value.

This Overview and Explanation provides a general outline of Debts and Assets for your financial awareness but is not presenting a complete list in entirety of all of the potential varieties of Debts or Assets.

"Charting Finances To Review"

Your Full Name:

_____

Social Security Number (Hers):

_____

Spouse's Full Name:

_____

Social Security Number (His):

_____

This Information Reflects Balances as of Today's Date:

_____

Charting One:

$ Overall Debt Review

Credit Card Debt:

Credit Card #1.

_____

a. Total Credit Card Balance for this
Credit Card #1.

$ _____

b. Monthly Minimum $$ Amount Due for this Credit Card #1.

$ _____

Credit Card #2.

_____

a. Total Credit Card Balance for this
Credit Card #2.

$ _____

b. Monthly Minimum $$ Amount Due for this Credit Card #2.

$ _____

Credit Card #3.

_____

a. Total Credit Card Balance for this
Credit Card #3.

$ _____

b. Monthly Minimum $$ Amount Due for this Credit Card #3.

$_____

Your Residence Debt:

Mortgage Information:

Name of Mortgage / Bank.

_____

Total Mortgage Loan Balance - Loan Responsibility.

$ _____

Or - Property Rental Information:

Name of Property Rental Management.

_____

Total Length of Property Rental Agreement -

Rental Terms. _____

Your Property Taxes - Liability, Annual Debt:

Property Taxes are Escrowed.
Property Taxes are included with Mortgage payment:
Yes or No

Property Taxes are Not Escrowed
Property Taxes are not included with Mortgage payment:
Yes or No

Additional Loan:

Home Equity Loan / Property Loan.

_____

Additional Loan.

_____

Charting Two:

$ Overall Monthly Operating Expenses

Residence Monthly Expenses:

Primary Home / Mortgage Cost per Month.

$ _____

Home Rental / Cost per Month.

$ _____

Property Taxes Cost per Month.

$ _____

Home Owners Insurance per Month.

$ _____

Renter's Insurance Cost per Month.

$ _____

Home Utilities Monthly Expenses:

Electric (Vendor Name).

_____

Average Cost per Month:

$ _____

Gas/Heat (Vendor Name).

_____

Average Cost per Month:

$ _____

Water (Vendor Name).

_____

Average Cost per Month:

$ _____

Trash (Vendor Name).

_____

Fee per Month:

$ _____

Cell Phone (Vendor Name).

_____

List the Phones on this Cell Phone Plan:

_____

Cost per Month:

$ _____

Home Phone (Vendor Name).

_____

Cost per Month:

$ _____

Cable TV / Internet Services (Vendor Name).

_____

Cost per Month:

$ _____

Security System Monitoring (Vendor Name).

_____

Cost per Month:

$ _____

Lawn Care Cost (Vendor Name).

_____

Cost per Month:

$ _____

Home Repairs Estimate.

Cost per Month:

$ _____

Transportation Monthly Expenses:

Car Loan #1
Make/Model/ Year.

_____

Cost per Month (His):

$ _____

Car Loan #2
Make/Model/Year.

_____

Cost per Month (Hers):

$ _____

Car Loan #3
Make/ Model /Year.

_____

Cost per Month:

$ _____

Auto Insurance (Vendor Name).

_____

Cost for all Cars per Month:

$ _____

Total Number of all Cars: _____

Gasoline Cost per Month for Total Number of Cars:

$ _____

Highway Toll Fees per Month for all Cars:

$ _____

Auto Maintenance and Auto Repairs
Per Month Average:

$ _____

Personal Care Monthly Expenses:

Hair Care Cost per Month:

$ _____

Nails and Beauty Services Cost per Month estimate:

$ _____

Clothing purchases Cost per Month:

$ _____

Dry-cleaning Cost per Month:

$ _____

Food Monthly Expenses:

Groceries for You and including your Children per Month:

$ _____

Restaurants Eat-Out per Month:

$ _____

Additional Monthly Expenses:

Gym Membership per Month:

$ _____

Country Club Membership Fee per Month:

$ _____

Other: $ _____

Other: $ _____

Other: $ _____

Other: $ _____

Child/Children Monthly Expenses:

School Tuition Cost, per Month:

$ _____
(Not for a Public school.)

School Sports Fees:

$ _____

School Lunch Cost:

$ _____

School Uniforms:

$ _____

Sports Uniforms:

$ _____

Extracurricular Lessons:

$ _____

Day Care Cost, per Month:

$ _____

Summer Camp Cost:

$ _____

Clothing Needs Cost:

$ _____

Child Medical Monthly Expenses:

Child's Medical Appointments average per Month:

$ _____

Child's Prescriptions
Monthly:

$ _____

Child's Dental Exams for 2 appointments / Year:

$ _____

Child's Orthodontics
Monthly:

$ _____

Child's Vision Exams / Glasses / Contacts:

$ _____

(Child's food expense included in joint total with Food
Monthly Expenses.)

Adult Medical Monthly Expenses:

Adult Medical Appointments average per Month:

$ _____

Adult Prescriptions
Monthly:

$ _____

Adult Dental Exams for 2 appointments / Year:

$ _____

Adult Vision Exams / Glasses / Contacts:

$ _____

Charting Three:

$ Overall Assets

Property Equity / Value:

Primary Home Equity: _____

Value: $ _____

Additional Home Equity: _____

Value: $ _____

Additional Land Equity: _____

Value: $ _____

Automobile Equity / Value:

Automobile Asset: _____

Value: $ _____

Automobile Asset: _____

Value: $ _____

Automobile Asset: _____

Value: $ _____

Banking Institutions, Asset Accounts:

Bank Name: _____
Account Type - Savings, Checking, Other:

$ _____

Bank Name: _____
Account Type - Savings, Checking, Other:

$ _____

Bank Name: _____
Account Type - Savings, Checking, Other:

$ _____

Bank Name: _____
Account Type - Savings, Checking, Other:

$ _____

Investment Asset Accounts:

Bank Name: _____

Account Type - _____

Total Value: $ _____

Bank Name: _____

Account Type - _____

Total Value: $ _____

Other Asset / Description: _____

Value: $ _____

Other Asset / Description: _____

Value: $ _____

Retirement Asset Accounts:

IRA Account - His Total Value:

$ _____

IRA Account - Hers Total Value:

$ _____

Company Stock Equity Total Value:

$ _____

Company Employee Bonuses per Year (Expectation):

$ _____

Life Insurance Policies Value:

$ _____

Social Security:
Account Credits for You and for Him:

My Social Security Benefits (Hers) -
The Year this will begin: _____

The Value: $ _____

His Social Security Benefits (His) -
The Year this will begin: _____

The Value: $ _____

"Charting Finances To Review"
This provides a general outline of Debts and Assets for your
financial awareness but is not presenting a complete list in
entirety of all of the potential varieties of Debts or Assets.

Disclaimer: Although this book may provide information and
opinions regarding the divorce process, this author and it's
contributors and Divorce Buddys do not provide professional legal,
financial or mental health counseling. Please consult a trained
professional for these matters.

Notes To Remember

Notes To Remember

The Smart Gal's

Researching

- Chapter 10 -

Today brings a new day.
What is true today is a true point in time.
And this day will go into your history book.

YOU know, what is true from YOUR days and all of
YOUR yesterdays.

You know YOUR truth.
You know where you have been spending your days.
You know all about your day-to-day activities.
You know how you have been spending your dollars.

Here is a question to consider.
What is the truth from HIS yesterdays?

Do you know?

His Truth?

Take a look at the past to make sure you have information

to consider this truth about His truth in your divorce negotiations.

Where has HE been spending his days?
And where has HE been spending your joint marital dollars?
Your "Soon-to-be-Ex"?
It's your marital right to review where HE has been spending your marital dollars. A marriage is a marital union, legally binding and joining together assets and debts as husband and wife.

Smart Idea to Check

Your Credit Check

We suggest that you may consider running a "Credit Check" on your credit history.
Look to see if there are unknown accounts, any new accounts under your married name.
Have accounts been opened?
Look for credit cards, for bank loans, for outstanding balances on your credit history.
Your credit rating.
When a debt is incurred during married years, the debt is considered a shared marital debt with shared responsibility. With the final Divorce Decree, the debts are divided and assigned to one spouse or to the other.

Debts Unknown

If a debt is left unknown, undiscovered or undisclosed, there is an element of vulnerability for the future. It is possible for a marital debt from the past to resurface in the future and become a new financial responsibility remaining from an old marital debt.

Also look into your credit card activity to see if there has been any supplemental spending. Seek to become well-informed.

Could there be any unfaithful spending? Spent on unfaithful relationships?

Paramour Spending

Here is another legal term, "Paramour."

This term is referring to a love relationship outside of the marriage. Defined as an illicit partner with a married person.

Any marital dollars that may have been spent on a paramour or paramours are dollars that may be recognized and compensated for in the divorce division.
Could there be past spending on paramours for travel, for dinners, for gifts or beauty services?

These dollars spent outside of the marriage can be reimbursed to you in the divorce settlement.

This information regarding a paramour can add a strong negotiating point in your divorce settlement.
With seeking to know the current state of affairs, you are better equipped with the truth for your divorce division. And this will bring a sense of awareness, knowing the extent of the losses.

With the division of marital assets and marital debts, the more you know about unknown spending provides leverage to reach a more favorable negotiation with the divorce decree agreement.

But it is our opinion, as Divorce Buddys, that we do not recommend a private investigator. It is too costly to hire an investigator. This brings an additional expense that brings more financial loss. Too costly financially and emotionally.

Take a look to review. You will feel better informed and may gain additional information for compensation in the divorce negotiations.

You are moving forward.

SM

Notes To Remember

Notes To Remember

_____

_____

_____

_____

_____

_____

_____

_____

_____

_____

_____

_____

_____

_____

The Smart Gal's

Parenting your Children

- Chapter 11 -

If marriage has given us children, we love our children.
We grow our children every day with loving care, and we
provide for their never-ending needs. Our children continue
to grow into adults, from our influences.

We are a creation of our influences and experiences.
As individuals, we have differing influences, viewpoints
and priorities. Often our actions are driven by our differing
thoughts and emotions.

Parenting Your Children

Our children are a part of us.
Parenting is a joint responsibility.
Yes, we all know it is best to parent a child with both the
mother and father.
When the husband and wife relationship comes to an end,
we are still forever parents to our children.
We call it shared-parenting.
The various influences of the human condition confirm
the need to create a joint parenting agreement in order to
outline the shared-parenting responsibility for the children.

Joint parenting may also be referred to as co-parenting, but we prefer the term "Shared-Parenting."

It is necessary to set-up an agreement to share in the parental responsibility, and this agreement is an important portion of the divorce decree.

For both parents this provides a legal document as the outline for sharing the parental responsibilities.

This is called Child Support, defined as how to support the child.

Both the mother and the father share the financial responsibility along with parental involvement.

Child Support

A Foundational Agreement

Within the divorce decree, there will be an agreed upon dollar sum for monthly child support. This sum is determined by a percentage of the parent's monthly income.

In Texas, the child support sum is dictated by the state, the OAG. The Office of the Attorney General.

Here we will assume the father is recognized as the Noncustodial Parent. Research found that in Texas, (at the time of this writing):

- For one child, the father will be expected to pay 20% of his income for child support.
- For two children, the father will be expected to pay 25% of his income for child support.

The state of Texas has set a pre-determined standardized order for child support with a pre-set bracket. But please be well-informed, this child support may be a negotiated sum.

You may seek to negotiate for additional financial child support from the child's father and ask to include additional areas of support within the divorce decree.

The total dollar amount of child support is important, but there are other areas of importance to consider.

Tracking Child Support Payments

A Critical Point:

Defining and determining the procedure for receiving the child support payments and tracking this payment history.

We recommend you confirm that your divorce decree states that every child support payment will flow through the state defined system, through the OAG, Office of Attorney General. This has a huge significance.

Over time, it is best to track and monitor every child support payment through the court system. Over time, life goes through ups and downs. Life happens and careers change. In the future, those child support payments may falter.

It is critical that the father is keenly aware that his monthly child support payments are being received, tracked, and registered to his child support account through the court ordered procedural system.

A Question:

You may wonder why HIS child support payments need to be tracked and monitored with the State Child Support payment system.

Our Answer:

Because over time, your "Soon-to-be-Ex" needs to know if his child support payment is late or unpaid, the father's payment history is being tracked. The payment history is being monitored. He is being held responsible.

What is the alternative to this child support court monitoring system?

There is an option for your divorce decree to allow court ordered child support payments to be paid from the father and delivered directly to the mother.
With this direct payment arrangement, the mother will be responsible to keep record of the payments. The mother will hold the burden to prove if any of the child support payments are late or unpaid. And if the child support payments falter, the only remedy is to return to the legal process with attorneys and fees. The legal process costs time, money and emotion.

For better protection, we recommend that within the divorce decree, the child support payments are designated to be tracked and registered through the state managed Child Support office.

On Your Child's 18th Birthday

Child Support Stops

In Texas, child support payments are required to continue until the child reaches 18 years of age.
This is significant.
And this is puzzling.

Because when a child becomes 18 years old, most are still attending and completing their high school education. The 18 year old child should still be attending school as a student. Still a dependent. I was shocked to learn the monthly child support is relinquished when the child reaches his/her 18ᵗʰ birthday.

By age 18, a child has not yet become self-supporting nor prepared for independent adult life. The child's financial needs continue but the father's child support stops. As a result, the continued financial expense begins to rest solely upon the mother.

We do not agree with this early completion date of child support to release the father's responsibility upon the child's 18ᵗʰ birthday. This release date meets the child support state requirements in Texas.

We recommend to include within your divorce decree the stipulation for the father's child support payments to continue through the completion of the child's high school education. Every child should have continuing financial support and parental assistance until the child has completed high school and graduated with their diploma.

Negotiate

Creatively

Within your divorce decree, child support concerns are negotiable. There is a standard for parental rights, but every element of the divorce decree is open for negotiation in order to best suit the needs of your children if you can gain agreement.

Here are Key Areas of Concern to Consider:

1. Consider to add: To share the expense for child-counseling, with a pre-set plan, structuring a pre-determined number of sessions. We recommend a minimum of 4 to 10 sessions per child according to the child's emotional adjustment.

2. Consider to add: To share childcare fees because the mother needs to be employed.

3. Consider to add: To share 50/50 in the child's extracurricular fees, sports fees, sports uniforms, sports camps, summer camps and sports lessons.

4. Consider to add: To propose a flexible agreement to share the children's birthday celebration day/time.

5. Consider to add: To share 50/50 in the cost for your child's student computer every 4 years for scholastic needs.

6. Consider to add: To confirm 50/50 in the child's medical costs, prescription costs with receipts.

7. Consider to add: To share 50/50 in orthodontics along with dental support.

8. Consider to add: At the time of the divorce decree, to equally deposit into a college fund a pre-determined sum to hold in savings for the child's future college education.

9. Consider to add: In the future, to share the cost of the child's wedding expenses.

Overnight Parental Responsibility

Suggestion: Not the Time for Romance

We know what's up ahead. Let's plan for it.

We can expect that most divorced parents will develop new adult romantic relationships in the future.
We recommend to state within the divorce decree that each parent will not allow an adult romantic relationship to remain overnight in the same house where the child is also residing for that night. It is beneficial for both parents to agree adult romantic relationships should not stay overnight while the child is in their parental care overnight. (Unless the parent has become married to that new spouse.)

Sharing Parental Care of the Child

An Idea instead of a Babysitter

We suggest, "First Option for the Child's Care".
Instead of hiring a babysitter to care for the child, whether the mother or the father plans to attend a social event or a business event, that the other parent should be the first option to care for the child. It is most beneficial to have the other parent care for the child when the first cannot.

Child Visitation

When Air Travel is Required

Over time, through the years, things change.
In the future, the father or the mother may desire to relocate their residence, requiring air travel for child visitation. It is helpful to think ahead to prepare for this potential issue.

Here is a creative concept for the best protection of your children.

Consider First Class Safety

If a parent chooses to relocate their residence and air travel becomes necessary for child visitation, it's best for the parents to agree for the child to travel in "first class" seating for their child's safety.

Here is our wisdom:
If air travel is necessary for child visitation, pre-determine that your child will travel with the attention of the flight attendants provided in first class seating. At the time of your divorce, most do not think ahead about the future of relocating and child visitation changes. It is possible, one parent may relocate for employment, a business promotion, a personal relationship or to live close to aging parents.

It is best for your children to travel to see the other parent and for the child to travel with the best safety considerations. A first class airplane ticket provides heightened safety for your child's air travel. The flight crew will be especially aware of a child's needs while seated as a passenger in first class.

It is creative and beneficial to include this first class travel agreement in your divorce decree.

Out of the Country Travel

Consider Family Trips to Remain within the United States

We suggest to consider adding to your divorce decree that both parents agree that their children should not be allowed to travel outside of the United States during their childhood years.

Consider United States Limits

When a child travels outside of the United States, the other parent loses all contact and all parental control.
To agree to this limitation on international travel prevents future conflict and concern. We suggest to agree to keep the children within the United States and not allow the child to travel into foreign countries. This may be agreed upon for a mutual parental limitation providing protection for both parents.

Sharing and Caring

Shared-Parenting will continue for years to come.
Both mother and father will find there will be differing priorities and differing points of view. Conflicts and issues will happen. Wishes and concerns will arise.
Sharing the parenting will require sharing decisions every year.

Shared-Parenting

As parents, there is so much ahead to share ...

- Education Issues

- School Events

- Extra-Curricular Activities

- Family Events

- Medical Issues

- Celebrations

- Child's Accomplishments

- Vacations

- College Plans

- Your Child's Wedding Day

It is best to pre-set these additional parenting agreements within the original divorce decree so that this has been pre-determined and agreed upon between the mother and the father. In writing. Agreed. Within the divorce decree.

Thinking ahead.

Moving forward.

SM

Notes To Remember

_____

_____

_____

_____

_____

_____

_____

_____

_____

_____

_____

_____

_____

_____

_____

_____

Notes To Remember

_____

_____

_____

_____

_____

_____

_____

_____

_____

_____

_____

_____

_____

_____

The Smart Gal's

Setting-Up

- Chapter 12 -

Throughout life's journey, we are living and learning, striving and trying, falling down and getting back-up again.

Consider and realize how a baby grows stronger with each step.
Take a moment.
Reflect on these thoughts ...
Consider how a baby grows and moves forward.
Just follow me here for a moment.

- Imagine a baby, see how a baby learns to crawl. As she rocks back and forth to stretch herself to move forward.

- Think of the 1-year-old, as she strives to take her first steps at walking, even though walking will be an all-new adventure for her.

- Consider the 2-year-old child, as she barrels forward with momentum keeping up with her heart's desire to run. Pushing herself with delight and optimism.

- Observe the 3-year-old toddler, as she cries over her fall but she is determined to get back-up and to run again.

At every age, it's time to reach and to stretch in order to keep moving forward.

As adults, we are still learning.
We should be learning. And growing.
And stretching in our adult years.
We are most alive when we are striving to stretch to accomplish.

Here, let's consider Hope, our divorce buddy.

Hope is getting back-up.
She is beginning again.
Soon to be running again.

Hope is inspired again.
To get herself set-up, step by step. And with every step forward, she will gain new strengths. She will gain new ground and take new steps forward. Stretching herself to get back-up, to learn new ways to run her life again.
Full speed ahead.

Wherever you are in the journey of divorce,
we recommend setting-up to rebuild life anew.

Many of us, during our married years, shared the family household responsibilities. Many of us allowed our husbands to take responsibility of the family business matters. Today, many of us may find ourselves lacking experience in the area of finances and account management.

Here is a smart guide to begin.

Now is the time to make this Your time.
To take new steps forward to begin to set-up ...
Your new life ahead.

Getting Set-Up

1. ### Set-Up your New Bank Account - Now

   While you are still married, we suggest opening your
   new checking account now, with your current married
   name. Your full name.
   Your first name, your middle name, your maiden name
   and your still valid married last name.

   An Example for a New Bank Account

   Example Name: **Hope Ann Smith Jones**
   (First name, Middle name, Maiden name, Last name.)

   With this complete name identity, after the divorce
   is finalized, it will be simple to update your banking
   account name. After divorced, simply delete your
   married name and you will be set to continue with your
   maiden name already in place. And to be prepared
   to carry on. Choose a new bank, one with credit card
   services. With your new bank account, your banking
   history begins now with your full name. Don't delay. Set
   this up now. Smart.

2. ### Set-Up your New Credit Card - Now

   We recommend to open a new credit card under your
   new banking account. Or you may choose a current
   credit card provider to begin your new individual
   credit card account. A credit card under your full name

including your maiden name along with your married last name.

An Example for a New Credit Card Account

Example Name: **Hope Ann Smith Jones**
(First name, Middle name, Maiden name, Last name.)

Even if you are only approved for a low credit limit, there is benefit for you to begin your credit-history now. No need to reveal that you are in the process of a divorce. Seek to begin your credit history. You will rebuild and increase your credit limit over time.
But for now, get that credit card open in your name, your full married name, while you are still married. After divorced, simply delete your married name and you will be set to continue with your maiden name already in place. Smart.

3. Set-Up your New Email Address - Now

   Valuable to set up your new email communication.

   Create your new email address with a name/identity you can plan to continue to use following the finalization of your divorce.

   An Example for a New Email Account

   New Email Example: **HopeAnn@gmail.com**

   This new email address provides the benefit of a new email address for privacy now, enabling you to use a new email address to keep your divorce correspondence concealed in this new account. Concealed and private.

Create a new email name that will be well-designed to continue to use with your future relationships. Begin to rebuild your email contacts now. Smart.

4. Set-Up Your Last Will & Testament - Now

This is a smart step of preparedness.

We recommend to move forward and update your Last Will & Testament now even before your divorce is finalized.

Why Update - Now?

You are currently married. Currently, your joint assets will remain available as an inheritance to your current husband unless you make a change to your Last Will & Testament now. While you are in the divorce process, he remains your spouse even though he is your "Soon-to-be-Ex." It is a benefit to have your assets newly assigned to your children or to other family members now. If any tragic accident occurs, if you have updated your Last Will & Testament, your inheritance wishes will be awarded to your updated beneficiaries, perhaps your children or other family members.

Once your Last Will & Testament has been updated and notarized, then at that time, inform your current husband that he is no longer a beneficiary on your Will. All is done. Updated and revised.
Why tell him? It is better that he knows that your Will has been updated and finalized without continuing an inheritance death benefit awarded for him. Tell him

this news AFTER you have completed your updated changes to your Last Will & Testament.
Planning ahead now.
Setting up is smart.

Now is Your time to set-up and rebuild.
Keep stretching and you will get back up again.
Don't remain stuck in the past.

Seek wise counsel, consider advice, gain new learning, take in new interests and grow forward. Yes, it's hard.
But you are ready.
Why stay in the past?
Don't hibernate.
After a season, you will stretch and you will find your strength again.

With every step forward, you will grow stronger.
You are ready to walk and soon you will be ready to run.

Yes, you can. Yes, you.
Smart you.

Disclaimer: Although this book may provide information and opinions regarding the divorce process, this author and it's contributors and Divorce Buddys do not provide professional legal, financial or mental health counseling. Please consult a trained professional for these matters.

Notes To Remember

Notes To Remember

The Smart Gal's

Empowering

- Chapter 13 -

Power-Up!
Empowering.

Weather Report

What do we do when we hear the weather report?
What do we do when we hear there is a storm on the way?
The storm is predicted and can be seen on the horizon.
It looks like the storm is going to hit hard.
And it's coming.
It's on the way.

How to prepare for a storm?

We prepare and plan for our needs.
We get equipped and strengthened for what's coming.
We buy supplies including bottled water, food staples and a reserve of batteries.
We think ahead to make good provision to get through the upcoming storm.

Weather Forecast: A Storm is Coming

Divorce can be, like a storm.
It can be seen brewing on the horizon,
seen on the weather map of life.
We know it is time to prepare.
We need to get ready.

So what to do?
Do all that we can to have the power supplies that we will need.

Here is good news for you.
You will feel stronger as you make your preparations.

Power-Up: A List of Power Supplies

1. Idea: Join a Gym.

    Yes, there is life out there. There are people out there.
    And those at the gym agree that exercise reduces stress,
    increases circulation and strengthens your heart.

    We agree with the health recommendation to set a goal
    to work out three times per week at the gym.

    This is a good time to find a new community.
    Power-up with a workout at the gym. You will regain
    new strength.

2. Idea: Release Emotions with a
    Professional Counselor.

    The counselor is a place for your thoughtful
    introspection.

To process through your grief and to uncover deep feelings.

We suggest counseling once per month.
Suggested for 6 months.

3. Idea: Consider Adding Vitamins.

   Vitamins are recognized as a good idea.
   Consult with your doctor for your physical needs and your medical considerations.

4. Idea: Adopt a Pet.

   A pet brings comfort.
   A dog or a cat can be easily selected at the local pet shelter.
   A pet is a comforter and a companion. There is a long-term commitment to care for a pet. Consider the expense of pet food and pet medical care, but the benefits make it worthwhile. Consider your lifestyle, but know that a pet will bring a new friend into your life.

5. Idea: Invest in Good Rest and Sleep.

   Experts recommend eight and a half hours for sleep per night for restorative healing benefits.

6. Idea: Tune-in to Encouraging Tunes.

   Turn off those old love songs from the past.
   Choose new uplifting music selections.
   Play and replay and sing along.
   We suggest these tunes:
   - "I Will Survive"
   - "Brave"
   - "Fight Song"

7. Idea: Make and Take some Me-Time.

    - Quiet Thinking / Reflection
    - Prayer / Journaling
    - Meditation / Deep Breathing

    A time devoted to peaceful deep breathing is beneficial.
    And a time to pray for direction. Also journaling your
    thoughts in a private diary can be beneficial to help
    release your emotions.

8. Idea: Select to Watch Positive TV Programs.

    We recommend America's Funniest Videos.
    It's always good for a laugh.
    And laughter is good for the soul.

9. Idea: Attend a Local Church.

    A Church is a great place to find new community.
    Always welcoming visitors. Offers new opportunities!
    A place to reflect and to think on God.
    To find new activities that will invite new friendships.

Weather Report: Lean in and Hold on

Into every life, a storm will come.
But with each storm, we lean in and hold on, and we get
through it.

Hope, our divorce buddy. She did it.
Hope jumped right into powering-up and getting her life
moving forward again.
Hope visited a few gyms in her area.

She gave it some thought and decided to sign up for a local gym membership. Hope laced up her gym shoes and stepped out there.

You can too.

Lace up.
Power-up.
Empowering, don't you agree?
Feel the power of hope.

Here is the good news report.
We know this storm will pass.
And when the storm has passed, we will find we are stronger, and thankful.
And we discover, we have grown more compassionate and a bit wiser.

Weather Update: A Rainbow ahead

The skies will clear. This storm will pass.
A rainbow is on the way.

You will see blue skies again.
Coming your way.

SM

Notes To Remember

The Smart Gal's

Forgiving

- Chapter 14 -

This chapter may be the most-costly and the most-valuable.

To Forgive

Because to forgive means to give.
To release the debt. To give up the account.

Forgiveness involves the decision to release an offense.
To release the hurts.
To give away the hurts that another has inflicted upon you.

- You did not want that hurt. (Yes, I know.)
- You did not ask to be hurt. (I know. I believe you.)

Continuing to carry those hurts can impose a power that can hold you down. The hurt can weigh you down like a heap of heavy stones.
It is as if those hurts are a heavy burden stored in your backpack.
Stones that you are carrying with you everywhere you go.

To forgive is to remove the weight of those heavy stones of hurt.

Yes, I am sure those hurts really happened. I am sure those hurts were unfair, unexpected and painful.
Yes. I understand. I hear you.
I have lived it, and I know.
But it's best for you, to let go of the pain. Unpack those stones you have been carrying with you in your heart and mind.

Forgiveness does not declare that the offense or offenses were understandable. Nor were they acceptable. But let those offenses be released so that you can remove the weight of the pain. To give that pain away. To give forgiveness.

God teaches that we are to forgive those who hurt us.

Why?

Forgive?

God is the maker of heaven and earth, and God is love. God's love and God's wisdom teaches us to forgive those wrongful offenses. Yes, those offenses were wrong. Terribly wrong.
Give those hurts over to God, and let God handle the rest of that story.

Here is an idea for you to imagine in your mind ...
Or maybe you will consider this idea in real life.

This is an opportunity to release the pain of the past.

Release the Weight of the Past

An Idea
Suggested: To Forgive.

Step #1

Put on gardening gloves and go outside to collect small natural rocks/stones.
Gather random stones of low value to use and to discard in this exercise.
The size of the stones to range from 3 to 4 inches.
Quantity of stones to range from 10 to 20 rocks.

Step #2

With your outdoor garden hose, rinse the rocks with water to create a clean surface. Let the stones dry outside, in the sunshine.

Step #3

After the stones have dried, take a bold, thick, permanent felt tip marker/pen.
On each rock, write a word to designate one of those offenses that hurt you.

Hurts can be caused from a wide range of offenses including:

- Hurtful Words

- Harmful Actions

- Financial Losses

- Broken Promises

- Broken Commitments

- Broken Responsibilities

- Broken Trust

- Broken Relationships

One by one, write a word, your word of choice, on each rock to represent the hurtful action.

Step #4

Begin to load the descriptive stones into a backpack, duffle bag or an old suitcase.
With your rocks labeled and loaded into your backpack, pickup your backpack of hurts and lift it, and carry it around with you. Walking around.
Can you walk with your bag of rocks, lugging this load?
Feel the weight of it all?
These stones of hurt are heavy, and they slow you down.
Those stones make everything more difficult.
They hinder your ability to move forward.

Step #5

Now, an idea to release these offenses.
Consider, loading your backpack of rocks into the trunk of your car.
Drive to a nearby public lake or natural body of water, a stream, ocean or river.
While confirming other people or pets are not in your area, unload your backpack. One by one. Throw your stones into a desolate body of water.

Throw each with your word of declaration that this stone is now released.

- To give up the pain of this offense.

- To release the hurt from that hurt.

- To be gone from your backpack. Every one of them.

- To choose to declare, this offense is to be forgiven.

- To affirm that you will not carry this weight
  from the past
  into your new days ahead.

Leave your hurts behind you, submerged in the natural water and now out of sight. Your load has been released, and your backpack has been emptied.

This symbolic exercise can be recalled time and time again. Forgiving often requires more than a one-time release.

Now, as you return to your car, take in a deep breath.
And place your backpack into your trunk.
Notice, the heavy weight has been lifted.
Your backpack is much easier to carry.
Your backpack is freed-up and ready to gather new life.
Now.
New space is available in your backpack of life.
Now.
New joys.
Begin.

There is a season for grieving.
But then comes forth a new season for release of the past.
This is a process, and it takes time. It takes a decision.

To lose the heavy stones of hurt.
And when we forgive, we prepare to make room for
new life ahead.

Welcome in a new season to move forward.

A valuable step of progress.
The step of Forgiveness.

And you are becoming more ready-than-ever to
move forward.

New days ahead.

Notes To Remember

_____

_____

_____

_____

_____

_____

_____

_____

_____

_____

_____

_____

_____

_____

_____

Notes To Remember

_____

_____

_____

_____

_____

_____

_____

_____

_____

_____

_____

_____

_____

_____

_____

_____

The Smart Gal's

Don't

- Chapter 15 -

It's better for all of us to find a way to avoid those mistakes that others wish they never would have done.

It's much better to avoid stumbling over a mistake that could be avoided. To take in good wisdom and to consider.
To know better.

Advice is the most valuable when it comes from those who have already been there. We gain from good advice. We trust those who have been there before us, and trust those who have already "walked in those shoes."

Here are some Don'ts that I have learned. Remember, I have lived this and learned this. And you may consider ...

Don't

1. Don't Stay in the Mud

Don't stay stuck in the mud.
Don't replay those hurtful memories in your mind
over and over again.
Don't retell your hurtful tale again and again.
The past has passed. Don't re-live it.
It will only hurt to re-tell your story, and it will keep
you stuck.
Get out of the mud and move forward.

2. Don't Lean on your Children

Your children are younger and less experienced than
you. Your children are not equipped with the maturity
to be your emotional support source.
Don't unload your hurts on them.

3. Don't Over-Use your Married Friends

Our married friends are true friends.
They are friends-for-life.

But our married friends have not lived the
journey of divorce.
In fact, we have found that most of our married friends
will remain in their "married-land".

Our life has taken a new change.
Over time, our married friends are likely to become
less connected to our concerns and less able to relate
with our life in the single world.

Your married friends are kind-hearted, but you cannot blame them if they do not know what you're going through. Your married friends have their married issues.

We are living in a new circle of life, the single life.

It's much better to seek a professional counselor to unload your questions, and fears and tears along your journey of divorce.

Don't expect your married friends to understand. Marrieds do not know what you're going through. Call a divorce buddy.

4. Don't stay Home Alone Every Day

Every Night after Night after Night

Seek New Groups

- Join a Gym
- Take a Cooking Class
- Attend a Church
- Try a Singles Event
- Volunteer for a Cause

Don't hibernate. There are new friends to meet. A new life ahead.

5. Don't Deliver a Letter to Your "Soon-to-be-Ex"

Don't deliver a nice letter.
Don't send an angry letter.
Don't give him a pleading letter.
Don't hand him a questioning letter, that asks, "Why?".

Don't give him a letter needing help.
Don't give him your hurts or your hopes in a letter.

Your "Soon-to-be-Ex" most likely has his own
torn-apart loyalties.
He has changed.
He is trying to figure out how to get HIS life
re-organized.
He has new priorities. New questions.
A new uneasiness. He is thinking about HIS needs,
HIS future and HIS best interests.

If you want to write the letter, for your personal
purposes, in order to vent, in order to put your
thoughts into words, then go ahead, write it.
But then tear it up and/or be sure to delete it.
Never mail or email that letter.

Don't deliver your thoughts to your "Soon-to-be-Ex".

6. Don't Yield to Your "Soon-to-be-Ex" ... Without
    A Trade for YOUR Benefit

Your "Soon-to-be-Ex" has HIS list of HIS wants.
And HIS wants are just as important as your view of
YOUR wants.

If your "Soon-to-be-Ex" asks for his golf clubs, stored in
your married garage, we can agree those are HIS golf
clubs. This is your opportunity to make a trade for an
exchange with him for your benefit. Agree to trade his
request for one of your desired possessions.

Gain agreement that you will exchange the possession
of an item in trade.

(An Example: In exchange for His golf clubs, ask to
keep possession of the kitchen table.)

Soon enough, everything will need to be negotiated
and everything will be divided.
Agree to provide for his current request
to gain an item in trade for YOUR benefit.
Don't give without a gain.
Don't yield without a trade.
Negotiate for a trade to benefit both while meeting
HIS request.

7. Don't Deliver Everything First

Wait until He Fulfills HIS Divorce Decree Obligations

The divorce decree is a mutual agreement.
Once the divorce is finalized, the document has been
entered with the court.

We Recommend:
Wait for him to satisfy all of HIS divorce decree
obligations.
Because ...

If you attentively and generously complete all of your
divorce decree details and expectations, then you
no longer have any leverage to pursue him to fulfill
all of HIS remaining agreed-upon divorce decree
expectations.
Wait until he has satisfied all of HIS payments,
delivered on all marital possessions and completed all
tasks and account closures. Having finalized with HIS
divorce agreements and commitments, first.

Why?

- He may choose to delay ...

- He may decide to avoid ...

- He can choose to become difficult to reach ...

After the divorce is signed and finalized, it is possible your "Now-Ex" may choose to disregard to follow through or delay on any point on the divorce decree. If so, it will cost additional dollars and time to take your EX back to court.

One avenue to enforce HIS lack of fulfillment of the agreed upon criteria in the finalized divorce decree is to file additional legal action against your EX. Costly.

We suggest to hold back until you are satisfied that He has delivered on all of His divorce decree agreements.

What To Do
Call Divorce Buddys

Call on us.

- We know what you're going through and what's up ahead.

- We provide guidance for women walking through the journey of divorce.

- We also provide personalized private and confidential Divorce Coaching by appointment.

Refer to the Reference Tools in this Guide-Book.

Plus ...

Visit Our Website	DivorceBuddys.com
Find Us on Twitter	TheSmartGalsGuide
See Us on Instagram	TheSmartGals
Follow Us on Pinterest	Divorce Buddys From Texas
Contact Us by Email	Information@DivorceBuddys.com
Contact Us by Phone	713-817-6217 Monday thru Friday, 9 am – 5 pm

Learn more about the various ways we are equipped to think it thru with you.

We are inspired to meet the need.
We are here to think it thru with you.

Smart thinking.
Smart you.

SM

Notes To Remember

The Smart Gal's

Moving Forward

- Chapter 16 -

The journey of life brings a few mountain-sized challenges.
Everyone has a mountain.

Don't you agree?

Challenges are delivered to each of us in a variety of
shapes and sizes.
There are a variety of mountain-sized challenges.
And many of us have experienced ... the mountain of Divorce.

Consider your heart.
Revive your inner strength of hope.
You can do it. You have the inner strength.
Dig deep. Dig up hope.
Find your strength. It's there. Yes, it's in there.
You're ready to press on to your next focus,
your next purpose.
There are new days ahead for you.

Why live in the shadow of your yesterday?
Why stay stuck in last year?
Why stay in last year's storm?
That storm may have put you into some mud.
If you are stuck in the mud of the past, you can choose to
stay stuck.
But don't allow yourself to stay stuck in the mud of
your yesterdays.

It will take some muscle-power to pull out.
It can be done. You can do it.

Put on Courage

I choose to put on courage.
To wear courage as if it is like putting on a beautiful blazer.
Yes, beautifully tailored to fit.
Just my size.
In my favorite color.
I put on courage every day and move forward.
With faith, hope and love.
I choose to forgive. I stretch to move forward.

Become well-informed, get better equipped, and
put on courage.
To live your life to the fullest.
This is life. This is your life.
And you are a one-of-a-kind.

In order to live your life and to experience your full potential,
prepare, get ready, and make a plan to move forward.

Moving is the act of relocating and gaining ground.
Moving in order to get to your desired destination.
Moving starts with realizing a desired destination.

Moving takes a plan to travel to that desired destination.
Moving requires work.
Moving takes muscle.
Moving brings change.
Moving brings progress that leads to your next place in life.
Moving creates a new vantage point, and a fresh viewpoint.
Moving forward.

Let's Get Going!

I have been where you are right now.
But today, I am a few miles ahead.

I'm moving forward. Every day.
And you are ready to move forward too!
To be fully engaged and alive again.
Set your mind to decide to move forward, and you will become
rejuvenated again.

- Re-Direct your Focus.

- Re-Discover your Interests.

- Re-Write your life's Goals from where you are now.

- Pray for how-to and where-to begin again.

- Re-Plan.

- Reach out.

- Re-Launch into your New Life ahead.

If you look from within, your inner strength will come forth
to the surface anew. Your natural instinct of courage will rise
from within.

Idea Part One:

Discover Your Plan on Paper

I have done this.
I have discovered my plan on paper.
Hope you will, too.

An Idea On Purpose

Go to your local store, to the office supplies section.
Buy a 16" x 22" Jumbo Paper Pad.
White paper, blank and ready for your discovery.

You could call this - Your think-tank.
You could call this - Your blank canvas.

At home, get ready to discover your plan.
Grab one of your bold markers.
Maybe a couple of markers in various colors.
Take a look at this blank page in front of you.
Say a prayer. And see what happens.
Discover the possibilities.

- What do you Love to do? Write it down.

- What are you Made to do? Write it down.

- List your Talents.

- List your Successes. Add them.

- List your life-long Interests. Remember them.

And see what comes to life on the page.
In front of you.

Discover New Plans

For you to consider ...

- ✓ Invite a new acquaintance to meet for a cup of coffee.
- ✓ Create a singles ladies group to gather for a book club.
- ✓ Start a new dinner-out group.
- ✓ Sign Up and attend a business course for training.
- ✓ Take a tennis lesson.
- ✓ Join a class for group dancing lessons.
- ✓ Team Up with a neighbor to exercise every Saturday for a power-walk.
- ✓ Begin a new computer course at a local community college for current development.

Moving forward requires Action!
All of these ideas, listed above, include action words.

- ✓ Invite
- ✓ Create
- ✓ Start
- ✓ Sign Up
- ✓ Take
- ✓ Join
- ✓ Team Up
- ✓ Begin

These are action words.
These all come-to-life, beginning with a plan.
Take action!

Idea Part Two:

Plan On It

Buy a new personal planner.
A New Monthly Calendar for this New Year ahead.

Open your new planner calendar to find each month.
Every month is on display.
Write your plans and your ideas on the heading for each
month ahead.
Add your notes and add your plans on the monthly heading.
To be on display for you to see in your personal planner calendar.

- Write in your calendar - Your interests.

- Write in your calendar - Your goals.

- Write in your calendar - Your ideas.

- Write in your calendar - Your inspirations.

- Write in your calendar - Your future plans!

Your plans will be ready to re-read, review and recharge you.
In the coming months.
Every month.

This is how to move forward.

And you will become a better You!
A smarter you.
As we live, we choose to continue to learn.
And with every mountain, we have the challenge and
the opportunity to become better.

When climbing over the mountain of divorce, we get stronger.
We acquire a fresh perspective, we gain in knowledge,
and we grow in wisdom.
We get through the necessary process of grief,
and we gain reflection and wisdom from this journey.

With time, we find our inner-strength again.
We learn to become more compassionate toward others.
We gain a better understanding and a heightened sensitivity
toward those who may be hurting.
We become better. We become even better!
Not bitter.
We grow better.

- *Today is your new day.*

- *Seek out your new plan.*

- *Create a new dream.*

- *Follow your heart.*

- *Help one another.*

- *Enjoy the little things.*

- *Laugh out loud.*

- *Be your best self.*

- *Cherish today.*

- *Dream big.*

- *Embrace new opportunities!*

New Days Ahead

You have a new life to live. Soon you will smile again.
Live, forgive and grow your life to the fullest.

Live on Purpose

Now get going. And hurry up.
And join me.
Live life again.

I am just a few miles up ahead.
Ready, Set, ... Go!

God bless you on the journey.
Moving forward.
There are new days ahead for you.

I will look to see you soon.

God lead you, and God bless you.

Disclaimer: Although this book may provide information and
opinions regarding the divorce process, this author and it's
contributors and Divorce Buddys do not provide professional legal,
financial or mental health counseling. Please consult a trained
professional for these matters.

Notes To Remember

The Smart Gal's

Reference Tools

Divorce Buddys

"Over 25 Key-Areas of Concern"

1 Car Asset Value vs. Car Loan Debt
2 House Debt vs House Equity / Asset
3 House Maintenance Costs and Repairs
4 Property Taxes
5 Credit Card Debt
6 New Credit Card Preparations
7 Credit Background Check
8 Temporary Support
9 Release of Cell Phone Account and Cell Phone Number
10 Adult's Counseling Expenses
11 Child Support for Childcare due to Mother's Employment
12 Child Support for Kids Summer Camps
13 Child Support for Sports Teams, Uniforms, Lessons
14 Child Support for Dental and Orthodontics
15 Child Support for Medical Insurance
16 Child Support for Medical Appointments and Prescriptions
17 Child Support for Child's Counseling
18 Child Support Extension through High School Graduation
19 College Support Agreement and Account for Child's College
20 Child Support for Child's future Wedding Expenses
21 Child Support to be paid through the Court System
22 Income Taxes and Child-Dependent Tax Deduction
23 Last Will & Testament, Create/Update/Rewrite
24 Alimony, Spousal Support, Career Re-Entry Support
25 Paramours, Dollars Spent
26 File "For a Reason"
27 The Mediation Process
28 Divorce Legal Fees
29 IRA / QDRO Retirement Plan Calculations

Divorce Buddys

"The 30 Most-Costly Mistakes"

1   Don't wait and don't delay to establish Temporary Orders.
2   Don't forget the benefit of Filing "For a Reason".
3   Don't agree to hold the Mortgage responsibility for the joint Home Loan.
4   Don't agree to a future sale of the Marital Residence. Get a Release now for sole rights for a future sale.
5   Don't accept the financial burden for House Repairs and Maintenance during the months of your marital Separation.
6   Don't accept the financial burden for all of Property Taxes during the months of Separation.
7   Don't accept the full responsibility for your Car Debt/Car Loan because this is a shared marital debt.
8   Don't wait to get your new Credit Card opened and established. Open your new Credit Card now.
9   Don't allow your married joint Credit Card to continue in-use. Consider to shut down your joint Credit Card line of credit before the divorce is finalized.
10 Don't sign until the other-side fulfills ALL of HIS obligations and financial commitments.
11 Don't sign your Divorce Decree until Your Cell Phone Number has been released and Your New Cell Phone Account is set-up for your continued use with the benefit of a new Account for your privacy.
12 Don't forget to seek compensation for Child's Counseling. For both parents to share in this Child's counseling expense.
13 Don't agree for the standard Child Support schedule to allow for payments to conclude on the Child's 18th Birthday. Add an extension for Child Support to continue through the completion of the Child's High School Graduation.
14 Don't allow your Child Support dollars to be paid directly to you. Best to process and keep track of the Child Support payments through the state's court system.
15 We don't agree with Interrogatories. Too costly.
16 We don't agree with the Deposition process. Too costly.
17 We don't agree to take a Divorce to Trial. Too costly. Negotiate before your case goes to trial.
18 We don't agree to hire a Child Advocate. Another cost.
19 We don't agree to hire an Amicus Attorney. Too costly.

20 We don't agree to hire an "Expert" for an assessment or opinion. Too costly.

21 We don't agree with the additional fees to conduct a Business valuation. Too costly and the results may be skewed and often contested.

22 Don't forget to determine who is granted the benefit for the Income Tax Deduction claiming the Child as a Dependent. This should be noted within your Divorce Decree.

23 Don't forget to negotiate for your Child's full range of additional expenses. Camps, School Supplies, School Team expenses, Computers, Cell Phone, College Savings, Child's Future Wedding Ceremony.

24 Don't blindly accept that everything is divided 50% and 50%. Everything is negotiable.

25 We don't trust your "Soon-to-be-Ex" to pay you later. Even with his best intentions, his motivation may diminish and his commitment may fade.

26 We don't agree to release the burden for Retribution Dollars for Paramour Dollars that were spent. Unfaithfully.

27 Don't go to Mediation without your Family Law Attorney. Have a list of your pre-set priorities. Privately review your list and privately choose areas where you are willing to compromise. While in the mediation process, to compromise in order to find agreement will save you money in limiting the continuing legal fees.

28 Don't accept full responsibility for YOUR-side of the Divorce Legal Fees. Negotiate for relief to help cover YOUR Divorce Legal expenses.

29 Don't forget to negotiate for Alimony. Everything is negotiable. Don't forget to negotiate for additional Spousal Support and compensation. For Career Re-Entry, Career Retraining, Additional College, Career Coach and Resume service.

30 Don't forget to negotiate for IRA Retirement benefits. QDRO. Research and calculate your Social Security entitlements.

Contact Information
Divorce Buddys

Sara A.
Author and Keynote Speaker
Certified Divorce Coach

 As a certified divorce coach, Sara knows how to guide women through the complex journey of divorce. As an author, Sara shares her experience and insight for women to become well-informed and make sure everything is considered.

Sara has been divorced and is inspired to help meet the need. She still believes in marriage and believes that marriage is God's best plan. Sara feels blessed to be a mom, and she knows the concerns of the single mom.

With her Bachelor Degree in Communications from The University of Texas, Austin, Sara brings experience in communications, innovation and concept creation. With a heart to encourage others, Sara was inspired to launch Divorce Buddys in Houston, Texas, in 2012.

Sara is a Keynote Speaker, available for speaking engagements at seminars and conferences. Sara is also consulting and guiding individual clients.

Contact Information for
Divorce Buddys Services:

Website   DivorceBuddys.com
Email   Information@DivorceBuddys.com
Office Phone 713-817-6217 (Business Hours: M-F, 9 am - 5 pm)

Sandra D.
Co-contributor
Certified Divorce Coach

Sandra finds much purpose in assisting women who are working through this divorce journey. Sandra is a certified divorce coach and believes in the Divorce Buddys concept to help guide women.

Sandra was previously divorced, and is now happily remarried. She has learned from the challenges of divorce. Sandra has a kind heart and recognizes the needs of the children as well as the adults. She is the loving mother of a blended family.

With Sandra's Bachelor of Science Degree in Civil Engineering from The University of Texas, Austin, Sandra has over 20 years as a professional Engineer and more recently an at-home Mom. Now, also a certified divorce coach, Sandra wants to help women through the divorce process.

Learn More About Divorce Buddys:

Website DivorceBuddys.com
Twitter @Divorce_Buddys
Twitter @TheSmartGals
Instagram @TheSmartGalsGuide

Contact Information

Sara A.
Author, Keynote Speaker and Guide
Certified Divorce Coach

Keynote Topics:

- **What Lawyers don't tell You**
  Become Well-Informed.

- **Divorce Dizziness**
  The Discovery, the Documents, the Details and the Delays.

- **Insider-Thinking**
  A Wealth of Information.

- **The Tennis Game of Divorce**
  How to Control the Back & Forth.

We all live and learn.
Sara agrees marriage is God's best plan, and
she celebrates marriage.
But most likely, we all know someone in our circle,
that has gone through the journey of divorce.
We can console, but most of us don't know where to turn.
Don't go solo.
Sara has learned through the journey of divorce.
Sara brings experience guiding women through.
To become well-informed.
With the potential to save thousands of dollars.

Divorce is highly complex.
But there are new days ahead.
Become well-informed.

The Smart Gal's Guide *thru* Divorce

Sara A.
Keynote Speaker & Guide

Contact Information

Email Direct Sara@DivorceBuddys.com
Office Phone 713-817-6217 (Business hours)
Monday thru Friday, 9 am – 5 pm

Notes To Remember

_____

_____

_____

_____

_____

_____

_____

_____

_____

_____

_____

_____

_____

_____

SM

Printed in the United States
By Bookmasters